Creating a Happy School Community

Bobbie Kalman

Crabtree Publishing Company

www.crabtreebooks.com

Created by Bobbie Kalman

For Rob Aguiar and his amazing class at Parkfield Junior School.
Rob and his students have inspired me in many ways while writing this series.
They are kind, grateful, mindful, and happy!
(See their picture on page 31 and on the back cover.)

Author and Editor-in-Chief
Bobbie Kalman

Editor
Kathy Middleton

Proofreader
Crystal Sikkens

Photo research
Bobbie Kalman

Design
Bobbie Kalman
Katherine Berti
Samantha Crabtree
(text and cover)

Print and production coordinator
Katherine Berti

Special thanks to:
Thich Nhat Hanh for inspiration of the poem on page 16

Images:
© Bobbie Kalman: page 29
© Roberto Aguiar: page 31 and back cover
© Shutterstock.com: Cover and all other photographs and art images

Library and Archives Canada Cataloguing in Publication

Title: Creating a happy school community / Bobbie Kalman.
Names: Kalman, Bobbie, author.
Description: Series statement: Be your best self: building social-emotional skills | Includes index.
Identifiers: Canadiana (print) 20190134437 |
  Canadiana (ebook) 20190134445 |
  ISBN 9780778767077 (hardcover) |
  ISBN 9780778767114 (softcover) |
  ISBN 9781427124180 (HTML)
Subjects: LCSH: School children—Conduct of life—Juvenile literature. |
LCSH: Respect for persons—Juvenile literature. | LCSH: Elementary school environment—Juvenile literature. |
LCSH: Etiquette for children and teenagers—Juvenile literature.
Classification: LCC BJ1877.S75 K35 2019 | DDC j395.5—dc23

Library of Congress Cataloging-in-Publication Data

Names: Kalman, Bobbie, author.
Title: Creating a happy school community / Bobbie Kalman.
Description: New York : Crabtree Publishing Company, [2020] | Series: Be your best self: building social-emotional skills | Includes index. | (provided by Crabtree Publishing Company.)
Identifiers: LCCN 2019023739 (print) | LCCN 2019023740 (ebook) | ISBN 9781427124180 (ebook) | ISBN 9780778767077 (hardcover) | ISBN 9780778767114 (paperback)
Subjects: LCSH: School environment--Juvenile literature. | Mindfulness (Psychology)--Juvenile literature. | Affective education--Juvenile literature. | Inclusive education--Juvenile literature.
Classification: LCC LC210 (ebook) | LCC LC210 .K35 2020 (print) | DDC 371.102/4--dc23
LC record available at https://lccn.loc.gov/2019023739

Crabtree Publishing Company

www.crabtreebooks.com   1-800-387-7650

Printed in the U.S.A./102019/CG20190809

Published in Canada
Crabtree Publishing
616 Welland Ave.
St. Catharines, Ontario
L2M 5V6

Published in the United States
Crabtree Publishing
PMB 59051
350 Fifth Avenue, 59th Floor
New York, New York 10118

Published in the United Kingdom
Crabtree Publishing
Maritime House
Basin Road North, Hove
BN41 1WR

Published in Australia
Crabtree Publishing
Unit 3 – 5 Currumbin Court
Capalaba
QLD 4157

Contents

Your school community

A **community** is a group of people. It is also a place where people work together, help one another, and share many things, such as buildings and transportation. Communities also have roads, parks, playgrounds, and other outdoor areas for people to use and enjoy. Your school is a community made up of people and places. What kinds of buildings, rooms, and outdoor areas does your school community have? Who are the people who share those places?

Walk through your school and make a list of all the rooms. Write down how each room is used by you or other people.

Does your school have a library? What kinds of things are in your library that students share?

How many classrooms are there in your school? Do you learn in more than one classroom? Is there a computer room? Which is your favorite schoolroom? Why is it your favorite?

What are your favorite outdoor activities?

Does your school have a playground and an area for sports? What sports equipment do you share?

Do you bring a lunch to school, or do you buy lunch in a school cafeteria?

How do you get to and from school? Do you walk, ride your bike, or take a school bus?

School community helpers

A school is an educational community made up of adults and students. Principals, librarians, teachers, counselors, nurses, food-service people, and custodians are just a few of the people who work in schools. Students who attend school learn how to listen, develop different skills, solve problems, and think in different ways. Students and adults work together to make school a happy community.

Most schools have several teachers. This teacher–librarian is giving a geography lesson in the school library. She also makes sure the books and computers are ready for students to use.

The principal makes sure the school runs smoothly.

This fourth–grade teacher is also a coach. He teaches students how to play sports such as soccer and baseball.

If students feel sick at school, they can go to the health room or visit the school nurse.

This drawing shows some of the tools used by a custodian at school. How do you think he uses each tool?

Write down the names of five people who work at your school. Find out three things each one does to make your school a better place. Then, make cards with a group of friends to thank them for the things they do to help students. Your school community helpers will be very pleased by your **gratitude** and kindness.

A happy school community

A happy school is one in which students and teachers are kind, caring, and gentle toward one another. At a happy school, students look forward to being with their teachers and classmates. They show respect by cooperating, listening, and accepting one another. Students work as part of different teams and share similar goals and **values**. They make friends and feel connected to others when they work and play together. They help one another and ask for help when they need it. Music, art, sports, and other fun subjects and activities are part of happy schools. Students love to have fun while they learn!

Write down all the things that make your school a happy community. Share your good thoughts and experiences with your classmates.

Important social skills

Social skills are the ways we communicate with other people through words and actions.

The following are some important social skills we need to use at school:

- asking permission
- being a good friend
- complimenting others
- encouraging others
- sharing materials and ideas
- taking turns
- showing kindness and gratitude
- recognizing our feelings and the feelings of others
- dealing with our emotions
- using good manners
- knowing that it is wrong to hurt others
- solving problems
- managing time
- knowing how to get along and work with people who are different than we are
- learning to be patient
- feeling confident
- paying attention
- following directions
- disagreeing politely

Be your best SELf!

School is more than just a place to learn about subjects. It is also a place where you learn how to be your best self and build relationships with other people. This kind of learning is called **Social-Emotional Learning**. Teachers call it SEL, for short. Becoming your best self means learning to understand and manage your emotions, make good decisions, set positive goals, and practice social skills, such as those shown on page 9. Learning these skills will help you worry less and feel better about yourself.

I listen with my heart and treat others with love. It makes them happy and makes me happy, too.

Life is awesome!

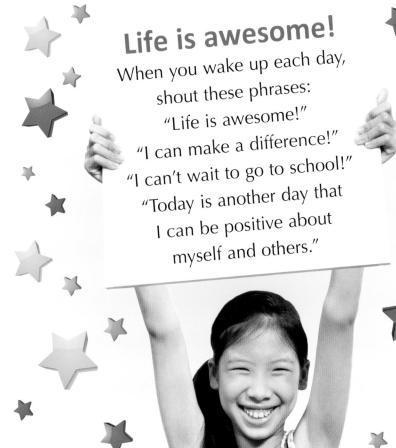

When you wake up each day, shout these phrases:
"Life is awesome!"
"I can make a difference!"
"I can't wait to go to school!"
"Today is another day that I can be positive about myself and others."

I love playing soccer. It is a great sport that makes me exercise and keeps me healthy. Soccer also teaches me how to play as part of a team. Teamwork is a very important skill we need when we play and work with others.

At school, we share rooms, desks and chairs, books, computers, and sports equipment. We also share information and ideas. We take turns speaking, think before we speak, and use our quiet voices. We cooperate with one another while we work together. We respect the opinions of others and help one another.

How does SEL help you be your best self?

Learning how to deal with negative emotions helps you have good relationships with your teachers and other students. Exploring what is important to you allows you to make friends with people who have the same interests as you. You can share your ideas and develop the skills you need to work with others. Practicing SEL skills can make school a fun place to learn for everyone.

Dealing with emotions

Some emotions make us feel happy, others make us sad, and some frighten us. Several kinds of emotions can visit us in a day. We can feel happy and then suddenly feel sad. SEL can help us understand why we feel different emotions and teach us how to manage them. Knowing how to deal with **stress** when you have negative emotions is called **resilience**. We can all learn to be resilient by changing how we think and react to difficult situations that happen to us. We can learn to **focus**, or put our attention on, being positive instead of being negative.

When I feel sad, I can give myself a hug or ask my friends for a group hug.

Ask yourself these questions

- What story am I telling myself right now?
- How am I showing my feelings?
- Can others see what I am feeling?
- What do I need right now to help me?
- How can I change my thoughts from negative to positive?
- What is my heart telling me to do?

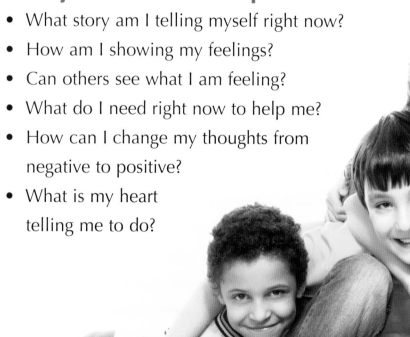

I can control my emotions by...

- counting to 10 and taking deep breaths
- writing down happy words
- remembering happy times
- writing a story or painting a picture of my feelings
- choosing friends who are happy and loving
- talking about my feelings with someone I trust
- walking away from people who are mean to me
- letting go of negative thoughts
- getting exercise, such as playing sports
- going for a walk in nature
- listening and dancing to my favorite music
- practicing **mindfulness** and **meditation** (see pages 16–17)

How can I be a better friend to myself? How can I be more resilient? Where is my happy place?

Ask for help!

If you have problems with difficult schoolwork, ask for help. Are there students in your class who could help you with schoolwork that you find too difficult? Ask your teacher for extra help after school on lessons you don't understand. If you have problems dealing with negative emotions or with other students who are hurting you, you need to talk to your principal or school counselor. Never hesitate to get help when you need it!

Empathy and kindness

Empathy is the ability to understand how someone else feels and to experience his or her feelings as your own. It is walking in another person's shoes. Think of empathy as having three body parts: a head, a heart, and a hand. The head understands what empathy is and what it does, the heart feels what someone else is feeling, and the hand takes the actions that are needed to help. Empathy is a very important part of getting along with others. It helps us know how our actions affect people, as well as understand more about the world around us. Kindness is an important part of empathy.

My mind and heart are open. Please talk to me.

My heart feels what you feel. Let me know how I can help.

Acts of Kindness Jar

These students have created a poster to show different ways their hands can help others. Giving support, sharing, volunteering, and donating are activities that show empathy.

*Using notes, you and other students can write **anonymously** about acts of kindness you have performed and put them into a jar. When you put in a note, take one out and read about someone else's act of kindness.*

Helping a student with a disability is an act of kindness that shows empathy.

If your friend is sad, talk to her and tell her you want to understand how she is feeling. Ask her to go for a walk or listen to some music with you. She will feel better knowing that you care about her.

You can sign up as a **volunteer helper** at your school to help younger children learn to read, use computers, or do other activities. There are many ways you can show empathy at your school. Ask your teacher how you can get started.

*These students are **brainstorming**, or sharing ideas, about what they would do if they were **refugees** escaping from a war, or if they lost their homes in a hurricane, tornado, or flood.*

- *What would you bring with you?*
- *What if you could not bring anything?*
- *What could you do to help other refugees who needed help?*
- *How can you help people in need of help in your school or community?*

Mindfulness activities

Many schools start the day with mindfulness activities. Mindfulness is being here NOW. It means paying attention to our thoughts, feelings, bodies, and minds in the present moment with interest, kindness, and calmness. Mindful activities include breathing, yoga, meditation, art, music, walking in nature, and thinking good thoughts, like the ones shown beside the boy on the right. Practicing mindfulness takes away stress and helps us be more positive and less negative. It also helps us pay attention to what we are learning. While practicing mindfulness, we become aware of what makes us happy and how we can help others be happy, too.

Breathing in, my breath goes deep. It makes me feel calm. I smile.

Breathing out, my breath goes slow. I feel happy. I let go.

When I breathe in, I am in the present moment. When I breathe out, I feel it is a wonderful moment!

Mindfulness starts with taking deep breaths. These children are breathing mindfully before and after their yoga class.

Breathing and meditation

Meditation is an activity that requires sitting quietly for a period of time and focusing on your breathing. It plays a big part in mindfulness. Meditation can help you let go of your negative thoughts and clear your mind. It helps you become more aware of what is happening around you now. When thoughts float into your head, chase them away by thinking of words that make you happy, such as "I love my life!" You can even hold onto a heart in your hands to remind you of happy, loving thoughts.

*Mindful yoga helps you build balance and strength. Yoga also helps reduce stress. This boy is doing a **Cobra Pose**. This pose helps you stay calm and gives you energy.*

You can become more mindful of nature by taking walks and using your five senses while you walk. What are...
- *5 things you could see?*
- *4 things you could touch?*
- *3 things you could hear?*
- *2 things you could smell?*
- *1 thing you could taste?*

Paint a picture to remind you of your nature walk. Painting helps you focus and be in the present moment.

17

Favorite school subjects

When it comes to learning subjects at school, we all have different favorites. Studying something you enjoy makes you happy. Which subjects are your favorites? If you like reading and writing, for example, you might become an author or **journalist**. If you like science, you could study plant and animal life or become a doctor. Learning about history can lead to many fascinating jobs, such as working in a museum. No matter what subjects you like, you could become a teacher who makes those subjects fun for students to learn! Your favorite subjects may change several times before you finish school. Enjoy them all!

Does art make you happy? What kinds of art do you enjoy doing?

What job might you like to have when you grow up? Would you like to be a teacher, chef, doctor, engineer, or musician?

You could be anything you want to be! Choose a career that you love!

Reading and writing

Reading and writing are two of the most important skills that you learn in school. By reading, you learn information on many subjects, through words written in books and on computers. You can also read stories, poems, and other creative materials. Writing allows you to share your ideas with others. You can share information, opinions, stories, poems, songs, and other kinds of written text.

What kinds of books do you like to read?

What do you like to write about?

Science and Math

Do you like figuring out problems and building things? Your favorite subjects might then be science, technology, engineering, or mathematics. Learning how these subjects work together and seeing how they play a part in our daily lives can be exciting! You can learn how to use science and math to help solve problems and make life more creative.

Social Studies

Would you like to travel to a different country, climb a mountain, or explore ancient cities? You can enjoy learning about them now! Social Studies teaches you geography and history. It also teaches you about people who have different **cultures**, or ways of life, in our **global**, or worldwide, community.

Fun ways to learn

Learning something new helps build our confidence. We learn new things every day. We learn from our parents, teachers, coaches, and friends. We also learn from books, the Internet, and when we take part in activities such as sports, music, and art.

- Which activities do you like to do best?
- Which ways of learning are the most fun?
- How do your teachers make learning fun?

Do you enjoy doing science experiments? Which senses are these students using while doing their experiment?

What kind of food do you think this girl was preparing long ago? How did she cook the food? How would you cook the same food today?

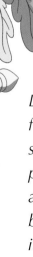

Draw a picture of a knight wearing armor.

Learning history from books is fun, but it is even more fun to see history come alive! Find a picture of a castle in a book and make a similar castle out of boxes. Write a story about what it would be like to live in a castle.

Are you a "maker"?

A **maker** learns how to do or make things by being creative. As a maker, you add fun to your learning! Makers often share their ideas, skills, and excitement for a project with other students. If you have a passion for games, fashion, robots, animals, art, or music, find some maker helpers and get started. The students on the right are making robots with the help of their teacher.

*These maker students are being creative by **mimicking**, or imitating, animals. They have painted their faces to resemble certain animals, and now they will write stories about the lives of those animals. They will then make a video, which will show how the animals move and what noises they make. Can you guess which animal each student is imitating?*

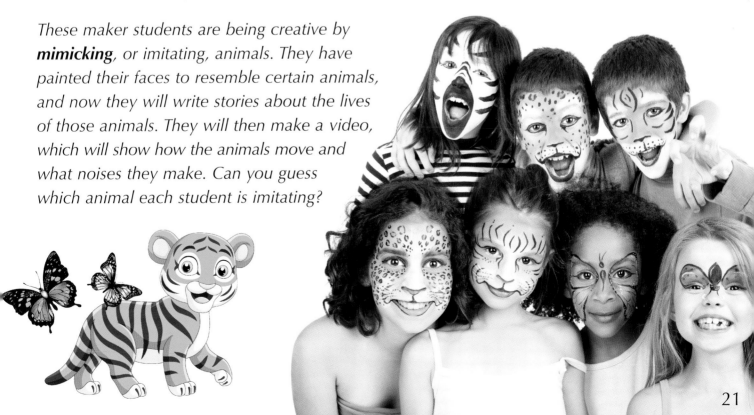

Music and art

Music makes you feel happy in many ways! You can enjoy music by singing, playing an instrument, listening, and dancing. Music creates a positive attitude toward learning and curiosity. Studies show that music helps develop both sides of your brain and makes you more creative. Music helps improve your memory, too. When you sing a song, you need to remember the words. When you play an instrument, you must remember the notes. Music helps your brain remember, but it also helps you forget your problems. Quiet, soothing music helps you relax, and loud, happy music makes you want to sing and dance! Music also connects you to your past. What happy memories do certain songs bring back when you hear them?

Being part of a band makes you feel connected to the other musicians. Being part of a drama class is exciting and fun! You learn to sing, dance, and act.

Quiet music calms me down.

Loud, happy music makes me dance!

What is your favorite kind of music?

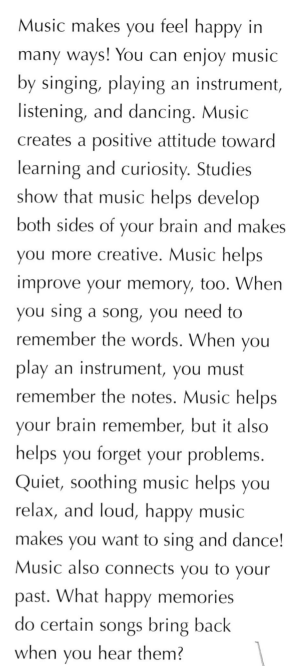

Art is creative and fun!

Adding art to lessons on any subject makes learning more fun—especially subjects you might find difficult. Art helps you develop your own ideas and makes you focus on how to present them. It allows you to express yourself in your own way. Art teaches you how to use pencils, paint, and to choose colors that best suit your pictures. It helps improve your memory and lifts your spirits. You can also use art to express your feelings when you don't want to talk about them.

With a group of friends, find some small, flat rocks or stones and paint pictures on them. What will you paint on your rocks?

Do you like painting pictures on rocks, or do you prefer to splash paint around in a creative way?

23

Physical education

Sports and games are a big part of school because exercise keeps students healthy and fit. Being fit means having a strong, healthy body that is able to do the things you want and need it to do. To be fit, you must exercise the muscles in your body. Your heart is a muscle, too. Exercise that gets your heart pumping helps keep your heart healthy. The sports and games you play at school are very important. Sports such as basketball, baseball, and soccer make you move quickly. They strengthen your heart and other muscles, as well as your brain. They also help you get rid of stress. What are your favorite ways of being active?

Team sports are a great way to build your skills at working and cooperating with others. A team cannot win if the members do not work together. These students love being part of a soccer team.

Healthy body and mind

Besides sports and fitness activities, physical education also teaches students how to keep healthy by eating nutritious foods, drinking plenty of water, getting enough sleep, and spending time outdoors. Students are also taught how to relax by practicing mindfulness and yoga.

These children are doing an exercise class in the gym at school. Their teacher shows them different ways to move.

*This girl is doing **gymnastics**. Gymnastics is made up of different exercises that help develop balance, strength, and **flexibility**. Gymnastics also helps you become more daring and self-confident.*

The children below are playing games at recess. What are your favorite recess games?

Student challenges

We all face challenges in our lives. Some challenges are bigger than others. Some students face big challenges every day. Physical challenges, such as not being able to walk, and emotional challenges, such as **ADHD**, can make attending school stressful. Children who have survived a war or lived in a refugee camp, have lost a family member, or faced violence at home may be suffering from **PTSD**. This means they have been injured physically or emotionally. They might feel sad or angry when they are at school. Bullying is another problem many students face. Showing empathy to your classmates can help make school a positive place for them. Your kindness can change their lives and yours!

*Children with PTSD, or **Post-Traumatic Stress Disorder**, might feel too sad or scared to play with other children. They may hide in a hallway and cry. You can help by listening, just sitting with them, or playing a game.*

*ADHD means **Attention Deficit Hyperactivity Disorder**. Do you or some friends have ADHD?*

ADHD makes it hard to:
- *sit still or wait your turn.*
- *stay quiet during class.*
- *concentrate on schoolwork.*
- *talk when you don't feel like it.*

Things that help:
- *mindfulness activities*
- *exercise*
- *having friends who understand and show empathy*

Does your school have areas where you can take quiet breaks or places where you can do exercises if you feel stressed?

Bullying is bad!

Bullying is a problem for many students. It can be...

- making fun of someone
- leaving him or her out of activities
- threatening, punching
- stealing from someone
- spreading harmful stories
- bullying someone online

Some children can use the help of other students with their schoolwork. Is there someone at your school who could use your help?

*Using cell phones and other devices, some bullies send mean messages or put embarrassing stories or pictures of others online. This nasty act is called **cyberbullying**. It can make someone's life very difficult! It is very important to tell your parents and teachers if you are being bullied! You can help someone who is being bullied by showing empathy and by not taking part in bullying activities.*

When students come from other countries, they may have trouble talking to classmates if they do not speak the same language. Taking time to talk or read with them is a wonderful act of kindness. You can make them feel welcome by inviting them to play with you and your friends. Read Bobbie's Story on page 29.

Diversity and inclusion

The world is made up of a variety of people. Each person is unique and different. We have different faces, talents, and dreams. We may also belong to different cultures, practice different beliefs, wear different clothes, or speak different languages. **Diversity** is the word we use to describe variety among people. Sometimes we forget that we are more alike than we are different. We all need the same things and are connected to one another because we all live on Earth. By welcoming diversity and having a variety of people as part of our lives, we can create a happy life for everyone. This is called **inclusion**.

The children above are standing on top of a map showing the continents on Earth. Getting to know people from different countries and cultures is a great way to learn about the world! Draw your own map of the world and name some of the continents and countries from which your family and friends have come.

How can we be more inclusive?

We can get to know one another! We can talk to one another and share ways of life through stories, music, and art. We can teach one another about the special clothes we wear, the foods we eat, our favorite celebrations, and what our names mean. We can make a list of all the ways we are the same. We can share our challenges. What are your best and worst memories? What do you like the most about your school?

*Many schools today have children who have come from almost every continent. Many years ago, I, Bobbie Kalman, was a refugee and **immigrant** from Hungary, a country in Europe. Read my story below.*

Bobbie's Story

I was nine years old when I became a refugee after fleeing a **revolution** that took place in my country. For many years, I suffered from PTSD. I had terrible nightmares about our middle-of-the-night escape through forests and fields, with guns going off all around us. Months later, when I arrived at my new school, I couldn't speak any English and, unlike today, my sister and I were the only immigrants at the school. We felt very scared and alone. To help me learn English, my teacher asked other students in my class to take turns being my teacher.

My classmates took me around the school, taught me new words, and included me in fun recess games. I loved making new friends and am grateful for everything they taught me. I learned English very quickly, and before long, my teacher told me I was a good writer. I must have believed her because, since then, I've written hundreds of books!

Being a refugee made me resilient, flexible, and opened the door to a fabulous life. As a teacher, I helped other immigrant children believe in themselves, adjust to their new lives, and feel happy. I helped them understand that their dreams could come true, if they were true to themselves. What could you do to show empathy to immigrant children at your school?

Create a happy school!

There may be challenges at your school, but you can play a big role in making it a happy place to learn. Our purpose in life is to learn about ourselves and others. School is a great place to do that! When you believe that each person is important, you can build a happy school community. Each of you can make a difference to those around you. The children below are holding signs showing the powerful things they can do to make themselves and others happy.

Which of these things do you do every day?

These statements will help you believe in yourself!

I am honest. I am kind. I am strong.
I am grateful for who I am
and everything I have.
I have a good attitude.
I am not afraid to make mistakes.
I enjoy doing the things I love.
I love trying new things.
Each day, I repeat three positive
statements that make me feel good.
I have fun with my friends.
I can make the world a better place!

Smile and *be* happy!

Be kind. Help others!

Be grateful for your life and say thank you often!

Praise people and tell them why you appreciate them!

Listen to someone who needs to talk!

Accept yourself and others. You are all unique and special!

Be a rainbow in someone's cloud. Make someone happy!

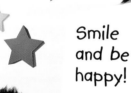

30

The children in this picture and their teacher, Mr. Aguiar, have done amazing things at their school. This book is dedicated to them (see page 2).

back row: *(left to right)*
Jesse, Rayyan, Minah, Mr. Rob Aguiar, Jay'ah, Mason, Shlok
middle row:
Farhan, Johan, Bilal, Abdulwareez, Faaiz
front row:
Yesha, Aisosa, Isha

Child rainbows!

The children in the picture above, called the **GLIMPSE TEAM**, are determined to change the world "through the eyes of a child!" They are warm, kind, and inclusive of one another's cultures and beliefs. Their hearts are filled with love, and they encourage one another to let their lights shine and know that they deserve to be respected and loved. By teaming up with authors and musicians, and with the help of their teacher, the students have put together several videos in their own words, and are helping make important changes in the world. If you want to learn more about the GLIMPSE TEAM, subscribe to their YouTube channel: GLIMPSE INTO THE LIFE OF A CHILD.

*The students helped raise money so that 15 children with **cleft lip**s or **palates**, could have surgery to repair the gap in their upper lip and give them beautiful smiles. They also helped raise money to make **Love Boxes** for children in hospitals. The boxes contain crafts, toys, books, dolls, stickers, puzzles, games, and other fun things for kids. Most important of all, the boxes are filled with love.*

Glossary

Note: Some boldfaced words are defined where they appear in the book.

anonymously Not identified by name

brainstorming Discussing ideas and solutions with a group of people

community A group of people who live or work together

culture A way of life, including food, clothing, customs, and beliefs

cyberbullying Bullying someone using electronic communication

flexibility Being able to bend easily

gratitude Being thankful

immigrant A person who leaves a country permanently to live in another country

journalist A person who reports the news

PTSD (Post-traumatic stress disorder) A mental health condition brought on by a very scary event

refugee A person forced to leave his or her country because of a war or natural disaster

resilience The ability to recover quickly from difficulties or negative emotions

revolution A war against a government

stress The state of tension or mental strain during difficult times

values A person's beliefs about what is important and what is right and wrong

volunteer helper Someone who assists elementary teachers at school

Index